TRY NOT TO LAUGH CHALLENGE

10 YEAR OLD EDITION

JOKE BOOK

Silly Fun Kid publishing

© copyright 2020 Silly Fun Kid Publishing-All rights reserved

The content contained within this book may not be reproduced, duplicated, or transmitted without direct written permission from the author or publisher

Thank you for choosing Silly Fun Kid

Silly Fun Kid is a nature comedian, represents the work of comedian friends, they try to send some happiness to the little stars and make them laugh and enjoy reading jokes.

Copyright © 2020 Silly Fun Kid The content contained within this book may not be reproduced, duplicated, or transmitted without direct written permission from the author or publisher.

Have a question? please visit
sites.google.com/view/sillyfunkid/books
or
use **QR Code**

to learn more and send us message.

We hope you have a great funny time with this book, if you like our books please support us with a review this encourages us to do more things.

Try Not To Laugh Challenge

 ## BONUS PLAY!

Join our Joke Club and get the Bonus play PDF!

 Simply type THIS URL :

https://sites.google.com/view/sillyfunkid/free?authuser=0

Or
use QR code

and you will get 20 best Funny jokes!
by Silly Fun Kid

Welcome to the try not laugh challenge

How to play the game?
The try not to laugh challenge is made up of 10 rounds, every round has 2 jesters, each player has a jester, and should make the second player laugh score to the points.
after completing the 10 rounds add all points and find the winner! "Master"

Round 11 : "THE ROUND GIFT"
the round 11 is the rounds gift which is the champion should get a gift!

Who can play this game?
the try not to laugh challenge is a super fun fast easy game for the family or friends to play together and get tons of laughs!

JOKESTER 1   JOKESTER 1

Rules of
The Try Laugh challenge

- bring the player's friends or family members, get your pencil, prepare your comedy power.

- determine who's the "jokester1" and "jokester2"

- jokester 1 will hold the book and read the jokes.

- pass the book to jokester 2 read jokes.

- once the round completed score points.

- the same thing until round 11, then add all points to find the champion!

- all these guides you will find on the bottom the pages after.

- give to the champion any gifts!

Ready! time to play don't laugh

JOKESTER 1

Why did ghost always sleep with the light on?   /1
He was afraid of scary ghost!

how the math book was crushed?   /1
with a heap of problems!

What do you call a little dinosaur?
A dino   /1

how does the race between a turtle and snail?   /1
It ended in a tie.

 JOKES TOTAL   /4

JOKESTER 1

what happened when the dragon watch a comedy movie?
he burned TV with laugher   /1

What did the gorilla say when he got kicked out of the zoo?
" Okay! ..give me my banana bag!!"   /1

Why do ducks have flat feet?
to crush out the annoying bugs   /1

how did the dinosaur get his driver's license?
he acted in many movies as a driver   /1

JOKES TOTAL   /4

pass the book to jokester 2! ➡

JOKESTER 2

How did the bunny become rich?
he wins 14 carrots.   /1

Why couldn't the scales weigh the butcher?
because he has a lot of meat!   /1

Why don't you get tired of walking with the wall?   /1
because there is a door!

How do bees keep cool?
They use bee-conditioning.   /1

 JOKES TOTAL   /4

JOKESTER 2

What if you fell into an icy lake?
nothing, your members will take a vacation   /1

If your cat talks English in the kitchen, what is talk in the bathroom?
meow meow language!   /1

Why are monkeys so intelligent?
Because they're always in schools.   /1

Why did the rat put his cheese in the freezer?
He wanted to eat ice cheese!   /1

JOKES TOTAL   /4

time to add up your points!

SCORE BOARD

In each jokester's add total jokes points for this round!

JOKESTER 1 _____ /8
TOTAL

JOKESTER 2 _____ /8
TOTAL

_____
ROUND 1 WINNER

JOKESTER 1

How do olives enjoy a day out?
They relish in it

___/1

What do nosey sausages do?
It gets sandwiched business.

___/1

what do you do if you see a superhero?
go to the supermarket

___/1

what did the dentist lose?
his teeth!

___/1

 **JOKES TOTAL** ___/4

JOKESTER 1

what did shark do in the morning?
brushed his teeth to eat some sardines for breakfast   /1

What do you get when you cross a cow and a salad?
hamburger!   /1

What did gorillas learn today in school?
not enough, they have to back tomorrow   /1

why did the pasta go to prison?   /1
they think thought it was noodles!

JOKES TOTAL   /4

pass the book to jokester 2! ➡

JOKESTER 2

Why are polar bears are not smart?   /1
Because they don't like schools!

Why does lemon have to put on sunscreen before they go to the beach?   /1
until does not become orange!

What do you call a cow on a rollercoaster?   /1
A milkshake!

What do you call a dinosaur with no legs?
I'm not scared   /1

 JOKES TOTAL   /4

JOKESTER 2

Why are ghosts are good in math?
Because you can see the solution   /1

what is the prize won by the cows?
best moo-vie of the year!
                                          /1

why did the witch fell off the broom?
it was not a broom but a stick.   /1

how do you know the octopus married many times?   /1
you will find 8 rings on his hand

   **JOKES TOTAL**   /4

time to add up your points!

SCORE BOARD

In each jokester's add total jokes points for this round!

JOKESTER 1   /8
                                 TOTAL

JOKESTER 2   /8
                                 TOTAL

_____

ROUND 1 WINNER

JOKESTER 1

why were ghosts screaming inside
the cinema hall?   /1
the movie was so scary!

what hobby do penguins like to
do?   /1
frozen fish fishing!

what did the girl zombie wear for
her birthday?   /1
a rotten dress

what do you call an old lady with
no teeth?   /1
a witch with no wish!

 JOKES TOTAL   /4

JOKESTER 1

how do you know that ducks always talk a lot?
They always quack quack with no stop! ___/1

what did the snowman say to another snowman?
I think it cold, let go home! ___/1

what happened when the dragon caught a cold?
he burned his neighborhood who live in! ___/1

what is skeleton's favorite food?
beef ribs, preferably grilled! ___/1

 **JOKES TOTAL** ___/4

pass the book to jokester 2! ➡

JOKESTER 2

what happened to the eggs when
they go to the amusement park?   /1
he was taken to the hospital because he
broke!

what was the dream of the princess /1
bunny?
to get married and go to the bunny-moon

why bees are so sweet?   /1
no, she not, she's just work in the honey
factory!

what do the sheep decide to do if
they lose the competition?   /1
will become bald!

 **JOKES TOTAL**   /4

JOKESTER 2

why did the ghost go to the doctor?   /1
he felt invisible

what did the snake say to the ant when sat on it?   /1
sssso ssssorry!

why did the pizza look pretty?   /1
because it so cheesy

Why did the chicken get a penalty?   /1
because they went to school on Sunday

 **JOKES TOTAL**   /4

time to add up your points!

SCORE BOARD

In each jokester's add total jokes points for this round!

JOKESTER 1 _____ /8
            TOTAL

JOKESTER 2 _____ /8
            TOTAL

_____
ROUND 1 WINNER

JOKESTER 1

why didn't the chimpanzee go to the party?
because it was the last episode of the beautiful gorilla series   /1

why mermaids are beautiful?
because they farting beautiful fart!   /1

what did the witch say to the fart elephant?
abracadabra stoop farting!!!   /1

why bears can't run?
because honey that ate it is heavy!   /1

 **JOKES TOTAL**   /4

JOKESTER 1

what did the dentist say to the pirates? ___/1
you should go to the car wash, and it will be washed well

what do hamburgers like to watch on Friday night? ___/1
a meat-ball

what is popcorn's favorite hobby? ___/1
watching TV

how do you know that the dog is hungry? ___/1
when his saliva climbs onto his face

 **JOKES TOTAL** ___/4

pass the book to jokester 2! ➡

JOKESTER 2

how do you know that the cat went
into a quarrel with its friend?   /1
see scratches on her face!

what is the difference between
unicorns and horses?   /1
unicorns they fart too much!!

where did cows go on Saturday
night?   /1
to the moo moo concert!

what happens if hen's get angry?
you will see feathers everywhere!   /1

 JOKES TOTAL   /4

JOKESTER 2

how do you know there is a mammoth in the kitchen?   /1
you see that the refrigerator door is not closing

how do you know that the crocodile is intelligent?   /1
he make a shoe brand

how do sheep wakeup in the morning?   /1
when the alarm says "baa-baa tik tok"

when father bull get angry with his son what he will do?   /1
nothing, will crush then will be into a meatball

JOKES TOTAL   /4

time to add up your points! ➡

SCORE BOARD

In each jokester's add total jokes points for this round!

JOKESTER 1   /8
                                 TOTAL

JOKESTER 2   /8
                                 TOTAL

_____
ROUND 1 WINNER

JOKESTER 1

Why did the snowman go to the doctor?
because he broke his carrot nose! ___/1

What happens if life gives you lemon?
the fart will become more acidic! ___/1

What did the bald horse say when he received a comb for his birthday?
Thanks, I'll never part with this! ___/1

How can you tell if a spider is a boy or a girl?
girl spider like to weave a dresses! ___/1

JOKES TOTAL ___/4

JOKESTER 1

why chocolate didn't go to the event?
no, she is just choco-late!   /1

what if rained banans?
we will become monkeys   /1

Where would you find a dragon?
in the place, which burned it!   /1

What's white and can't fly?
A fridge!   /1

 **JOKES TOTAL**   /4

pass the book to jokester 2! ➡

JOKESTER 2

How do you talk to a mammoth?
Use BIG words! ___/1

What has three letters and scratches you?
An angry cat! ___/1

Why do birds fly?
because walking makes them lazy! ___/1

Why do pencils always win the game?
Because they have the most points! ___/1

 JOKES TOTAL ___/4

JOKESTER 2

Why did the farmer ride his horse /1
into town?
to take him to the doctor he has diarrhea!

what do you call a sandwich with /1
no meat?
bread!

what is the witch wich?   /1
to had broom last generation!

Which side of a lion has the most /1
hair?
The outside!

JOKES TOTAL ____ /4

time to add up your points!

SCORE BOARD

In each jokester's add total jokes points for this round!

JOKESTER 1

___/8
TOTAL

JOKESTER 2

___/8
TOTAL

_____
ROUND 1 WINNER

JOKESTER 1

What if rained candy?
The teeth will become extinct! ___/1

How many days have a week?
5 boring days and 2 fun days! ___/1

Why did the pirates go to school?
Because they wanted to be a Smart! ___/1

What did one cockroach say to his friend?
Should we walk or catch a rat? ___/1

 **JOKES TOTAL** ___/4

JOKESTER 1

What do you call a sleeping dog?
a drool!
___/1

What do you call a cat clinging to you?
pasting cat!
___/1

how did the monkey open the door?
with his mon-key!
___/1

What's the dumbest animal in the jungle?
antarctic fly!
___/1

 **JOKES TOTAL** ___/4

pass the book to jokester 2! ➡

JOKESTER 2

What did the snake say in the winter?   /1
it's ssssnowing

What did the cheese say to the cat?   /1
Nothing, cheese can't talk!

Why were cheetahs expelled from the amusement park?   /1
because they cheaters!

Why did the gorilla jump on his potato plants?   /1
He wanted to eat mashed potatoes!

JOKES TOTAL   /4

JOKESTER 2

What did the fish say when he bumped into a shark? ____/1
sorry I'm not a fish!

Why did the puppy go to the doctor? ____/1
Because he was the doctor's pet!

What did number one say to another number one in the gym? ____/1
we are two tired!

What do you get when you cross 100 sheep? ____/1
a pile of wool!

 **JOKES TOTAL** ____/4

time to add up your points!

SCORE BOARD

In each jokester's add total jokes points for this round!

JOKESTER 1

_____ /8
TOTAL

JOKESTER 2

_____ /8
TOTAL

_____
ROUND 1 WINNER

JOKESTER 1

Where did the triangle and the circle go?
to the shapes party!   /1

Why did the skeleton break his bone?
he was trying to dance a ballet dance!   /1

Where do you find a cheetah with no legs?
Right where you left him!   /1

Can February fly?
yes, every year
    /1

 JOKES TOTAL   /4

JOKESTER 1

What did the chimpanzee bring when he see the giraffe?
a ladder!

___/1

Why did the ghost enter the freezer?
he wanted to be a cold ghost!

___/1

What is the fastest thing in the morning?
break-fast!

___/1

What type of haircut do cheep get?
baa-baacuts!

___/1

JOKES TOTAL ___/4

pass the book to jokester 2! ➡

JOKESTER 2

What did gold-fish say to the starfish?
I'm so expensive!

/1

what did potatoes say to the ketchup?
let's get some chips

/1

what is lions' favorite hobby?
nothing, just some grilled meat at the weekend

/1

why didn't dinosaur go to school?
he had a diarrhea!

/1

 **JOKES TOTAL** /4

JOKESTER 2

why did the zombie felt rotten?
he ate spoiled cheese! /1

how did the spider become famous?
he was walking on the TV screen /1

where did mosquitos go at midnight?
to anyone people! /1

what did the toilet say to another toilet when they went to the dirty party? /1
wow! you look soo stinky!

 **JOKES TOTAL** /4

time to add up your points!

SCORE BOARD

In each jokester's add total jokes points for this round!

JOKESTER 1   ___/8
                                               TOTAL

JOKESTER 2   ___/8
                                               TOTAL

_____

ROUND 1 WINNER

JOKESTER 1

why did pigeons click the man's head?   /1
nothing, he just find some bread!

what did the father ghost say to the mother ghost on graduation day?   /1
this my daughter, she looks so scary!

why does the turtle not speed?
because the slow is his passion!   /1

Why did the tomato blush?
no, he put so much makeup!

/1

 JOKES TOTAL   /4

JOKESTER 1

why did bears like to go to school?
because they like to hear stories of fart

/1

how do you know there is a gorilla in your home?
when bananas disappear!

/1

what kind of chairs do chickens like to sit in?
eggs chair!

/1

Why can't the chimpanzee sit in front of the elephant in school.
Because his feet were SO smelly!

/1

 **JOKES TOTAL**   /4

pass the book to jokester 2! ➡

JOKESTER 2

why was the dinosaur expelled from the test? /1
because he farted without warning!

what did the pen say to the pencil? /1
let's slide on the paper

Why are frogs do not alarmed? /1
Because they eat whatever bugs them!

what do you call a rainbow with no colors? /1
bow!

 JOKES TOTAL /4

JOKESTER 2

What do you call a witch that tells the time?   /1
A watch-witch!

how did the farmer know that the cows go into a quarrel last night? /1
he found milk became yogurt!

What do you call a fly dragon with no wings?   /1
A walking dinosaur!

What is green and yellow and brown and some black?   /1
a chameleon changes her clothes that she did not like!

JOKES TOTAL   /4

time to add up your points!

SCORE BOARD

In each jokester's add total jokes points for this round!

JOKESTER 1 _____ /8
            TOTAL

JOKESTER 2 _____ /8
            TOTAL

_____
ROUND 1 WINNER

JOKESTER 1

Why can't the princess play soccer?
Because she's always running away from the ball!   /1

What did pigs eat for breakfast?
dung pie!   /1

What happened when the motorcycle was invented?
he burned road with his farting!   /1

What's the best thing to put into a hamburger?
Your teeth!   /1

 **JOKES TOTAL**   /4

JOKESTER 1

Why are Superhero's suits so tight?
They're all size 'S'!   /1

What message is written at the door of the bees?
There is no honey!   /1

Where did monsters go on Friday night?
To the ogre dinner party!   /1

What do you get when you cross a dinosaur and a mammoth?
A disaster....RUN!   /1

 **JOKES TOTAL**   /4

pass the book to jokester 2! ➡

JOKESTER 2

Why are robots don't cry?
They have the heart of steel! /1

what is the song do fish like when they lay down on the pan?
fishshsh! fishshsh! /1

What is a witch's favorite book?
the magic book of farting! /1

What is a thing that cannot freeze?
the mind of the fly, because he's too stinky! /1

 **JOKES TOTAL** /4

JOKESTER 2

why did the bunny get the problem? /1
because he entered the math book to steal the carrots

how do you know there is a mummy at home? /1
if you don't find toilet paper!

What does one book say to another book in the winter? /1
It's cold Put on a jacket!

why did flies get a shower? /1
to participates in the competition for cleanest animal

 JOKES TOTAL /4

time to add up your points!

SCORE BOARD

In each jokester's add total jokes points for this round!

JOKESTER 1   /8
                                     TOTAL

JOKESTER 2   /8
                                     TOTAL

_____

ROUND 1 WINNER

JOKESTER 1

Why are dolls never eat?
because she hates opening her mouth   /1

What kind of dinner do moms never prepare in the evening?
breakfast!   /1

Did you hear the joke about the door?
Never mind, it had opened!   /1

What's the difference between a piano and a fish?
the piano launch musical notes but the fish launch fart bubbles   /1

 **JOKES TOTAL**   /4

JOKESTER 1

What did the washing machine say to the baby clothes?
You look too stinky!   /1

Why did the mummy break her leg?
She was trying a wrap!   /1

What is sneaking in the night surprise you in the morning in winter?
snow!   /1

Why did ghosts disappear?
no, they just playing hide and seek   /1

 JOKES TOTAL   /4

pass the book to jokester 2! ➡

JOKESTER 2

What did the cow say to her calf on his birthday? ___/1
It's moo-moo birthday!

What was the first animal in space? ___/1
The gorilla that jumped over the moon.

Why don't horses chew gum? ___/1
They do, just not in public.

Why didn't the farmer find his animals on 31 December? ___/1
no, they just go to the new year party!

 **JOKES TOTAL** ___/4

JOKESTER 2

What did the ocean say to the boat?
Nothing, it just waved.

/1

Why don't pirates shower?
no, they just like to take shower with the waves of the sea!

/1

How do zombies know that they are zombies?
They think, therefore they too rotten!

/1

What song does a rat like best?
Three Blind cheese

/1

 **JOKES TOTAL** /4

time to add up your points!

SCORE BOARD

In each jokester's add total jokes points for this round!

JOKESTER 1   _____/8
                       TOTAL

JOKESTER 2   _____/8
                       TOTAL

_____
ROUND 1 WINNER

ROUND

11

ROUND GIFT

JOKESTER 1

Why are ghosts good at video games?
Because they don't have lives!   /1

What did the cat say when he fell off the tree?
"Me-ow."   /1

What does a witch use to do her hair?
magic spell   /1

Can a chimpanzee jump higher than Mount Everest?
Yes, because a building can't jump at all.   /1

JOKES TOTAL   /4

JOKESTER 1

are there any similarities between Turkey and a monkey?
yes, they have keys!   /1

Where does a zombie keep his money?
In a toilet bank!   /1

How can you tell which sheep is the oldest in a group?
Just look for the grizzly.   /1

What happened when the dragon met his dreams?
he burned them!   /1

 **JOKES TOTAL**   /4

pass the book to jokester 2! ➡

JOKESTER 2

What did one colored chameleon say to the other?
Heard any good yolks lately? ___/1

what is the gift that the rabbit gave to his wife?
14 carrot gold. ___/1

how was the robber arrested in the neighborhood?
the smart old lady hit him with her cane! ___/1

why did the ant bring a ladder to school?
Because she wanted to go to high school. ___/1

 JOKES TOTAL ___/4

JOKESTER 2

why you can't tell eggs a big joke?   /1
because laugher will break them

How do you get a gorilla to like you?   /1
Act like a banana

why can't penguins throw jokes on ice?   /1
will melt!

what are the favorite hobbies of flies?   /1
telling stinky jokes!

 **JOKES TOTAL**   /4

time to add up your points!

SCORE BOARD

In each jokester's add total jokes points for this round!

JOKESTER 1 _____ /8
TOTAL

JOKESTER 2 _____ /8
TOTAL

_____
ROUND 1 WINNER

FINAL SCORE BOARD

	jokester 1 /8	jokester 2 /8
Round 1		
Round 2		
Round 3		
Round 4		
Round 5		
Round 6		
Round 7		
Round 8		
Round 9		
Round 10		
Round 11		
Total		

THE CHAMPION IS:

_____

Congradulation!

CHEK OUT OUR

Visit our Amazon store at:

OTHER JOKE BOOKS!

www.Amazon.com/author/sillyfunkid

Printed in the USA
CPSIA information can be obtained
at www.ICGtesting.com
LVHW021133091223
766108LV00009B/91

9 798584 421229